1982
A LIFE TO REMEMBER

A Little Something Yours

TIME TRAVEL

Looking for a gift as unforgettable as it is irresistible? Say hello to **1982: *A LIFE TO REMEMBER!*** *This isn't just a book—it's a time machine wrapped in stories, ready to whisk your loved ones back to a world bursting with resilience, change, and surprising moments.*

Picture 1982: a rollercoaster of grit and glory—America's national pride, Britain rebuilding, Canada flourishing, and Australia proving it could take on anything. Whether you're diving into groundbreaking events or meeting the unsung heroes who quietly shaped history, this book delivers all the drama, humor, and "I didn't know that!" surprises that will keep readers hooked.

But it doesn't stop there! This isn't just a sit-and-read experience—it's packed with trivia quizzes to stump even the family know-it-all and clever matching games for a fun, nostalgic trip down memory lane. History has never been this interactive or entertaining.

Perfect for history lovers, curious minds, or anyone who delights in uncovering hidden gems from the past, **1982: *A LIFE TO REMEMBER!*** *is your ticket to a meaningful and memorable gift. Because some years are just too special not to share.*

CHAPTER 1

IN THE NEWS

1.1 EVENTS THAT SHOCKED AND SHAPED THE WORLD IN 1982

THE FALKLANDS WAR: A CLASH OF NATIONS

On a cool April morning, word spread that Argentine forces had set foot on the Falkland Islands, stirring a storm of conflict with the United Kingdom over these lonely yet deeply cherished lands. For countless people, the war carried not just disputes over territory but echoes of pride and old imperial shadows. The rugged islands, shaped by relentless winds, became a stage for a tragic 10-week struggle. Both sides mourned fallen lives, while the world debated with uneasy voices. The war left marks not only on those who fought but also on humanity's collective memory, revealing sovereignty's true price.

THE FALKLANDS WAR: A CLASH OF NATIONS

THE SABRA AND SHATILA MASSACRE: SHADOWS OF WAR

In the heart of war-scarred Lebanon, September arrived with horror that echoed across the world. Within the Sabra and Shatila refugee camps, the massacre of Palestinian civilians unfolded under the dark shadow of the relentless Lebanese Civil War. The world looked on in anguish as reports and haunting images emerged, revealing the grim aftermath. This sorrowful chapter became a somber reminder of the fragility of the displaced and the harsh, unyielding realities carved by the weight of geopolitics.

TYLENOL MURDERS: FEAR IN A CAPSULE

In the autumn of 1982, America faced an unseen danger as the Tylenol murders cast a dark shadow over Chicago. Seven unsuspecting souls consumed cyanide-laced capsules, their lives tragically cut short. The heartbreak went beyond the deaths, shaking the nation's trust in everyday products. Families inspected labels with new caution, stores secured medicines, and tamper-proof packaging emerged. These haunting events became a solemn reminder of vigilance and innovations born painfully from tragedy.

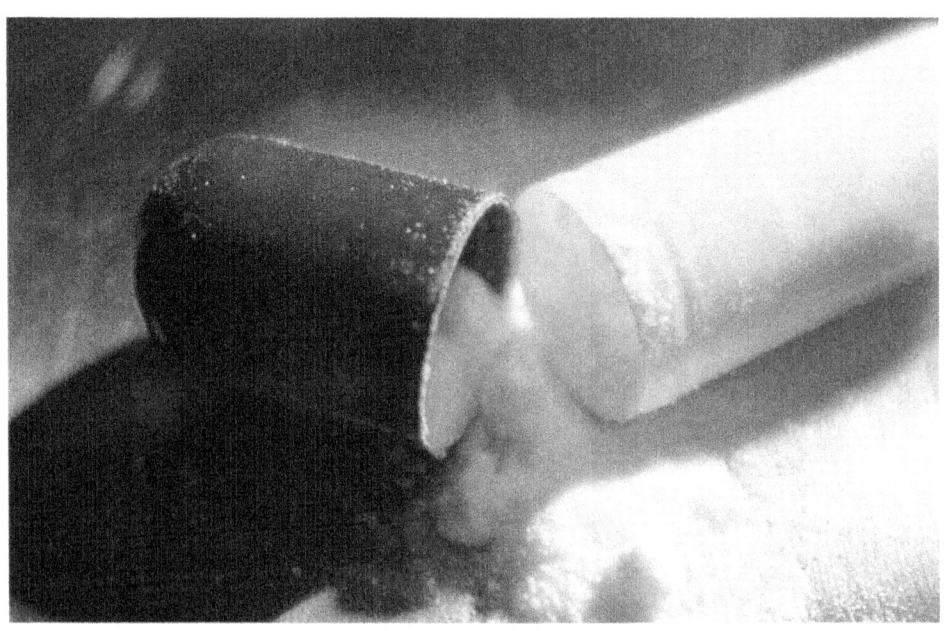

AIR FLORIDA FLIGHT 90: TRAGEDY ON THE POTOMAC

January 13, 1982, opened as an icy morning in Washington, D.C., yet few foresaw the sorrow about to unfold. Air Florida Flight 90, heavy with passengers, faltered after takeoff and plunged into the frozen Potomac River. The crash claimed 78 lives, leaving only a handful of survivors. Amid the despair, the bravery of bystanders—especially one man who plunged repeatedly into the icy waters to save others—etched a timeless story of humanity against the starkness of that devastating winter day.

BEAUNE COACH CRASH: FRANCE MOURNS ITS CHILDREN

Summer grew heavy with sorrow in France when a fiery crash on July 31 claimed 53 lives, most of them schoolchildren. A joyful holiday journey turned into a national heartbreak as grieving families and a shocked nation struggled to comprehend the depth of the loss. It stood as a poignant reminder of life's fragility and the need for greater road safety.

IRA BOMBINGS: TERROR IN LONDON

The summer of 1982 was darkened by the thunderous roar of explosions in London's Hyde Park and Regent's Park. The Provisional IRA's bombings struck at military personnel, claiming 11 lives and injuring many more. These attacks echoed the bitter tensions of Northern Ireland reaching into England's heart, leaving a city unsettled and a nation bound together in shared grief.

PAN AM FLIGHT 759: DISASTER IN LOUISIANA

On a sweltering July day, heartbreak struck Kenner, Louisiana, when Pan Am Flight 759 crashed into a quiet suburban neighborhood just after takeoff. The disaster claimed 145 lives on board and eight more on the ground. Amid the wreckage, stories of community strength surfaced, as neighbors united to aid survivors and bring comfort to grieving families.

EXECUTION OF KHALID ISLAMBOULI: JUSTICE OR VENGEANCE?

The execution of Khalid Islambouli, the man behind Egyptian President Anwar Sadat's assassination, sent ripples through the region. For some, it marked the end of a sorrowful chapter; for others, it widened the rifts within an already fragile Middle East. This act of retribution stood as a reminder of the tangled threads of justice and politics.

1.2 LEADERS AND POLITICS: MOVERS AND SHAKERS OF 1982

A NEW FACE FOR THE UNITED NATIONS

The year's dawn opened a hopeful chapter for the United Nations as Javier Pérez de Cuéllar, an experienced diplomat from Peru, assumed the role of Secretary-General on January 1. His appointment marked the first time a Latin American held the position, a symbolic stride toward global unity. Amid the shadow of Cold War tensions, Pérez de Cuéllar became a calming presence, devoted to mediating conflicts and advocating peace. His determination to bridge divides inspired cautious optimism, reminding the world that even in uncertain times, diplomacy still held the promise of meaningful change.

THE EQUAL RIGHTS AMENDMENT FALTERS

In the United States, the deadline for ratifying the Equal Rights Amendment (ERA) quietly passed in 1982, leaving a bittersweet imprint on the feminist movement. Despite decades of tireless campaigning and a wave of passionate support, the amendment fell short of the necessary state ratifications. For many, this moment stood as a solemn reminder of the struggles still confronting women seeking legal equality. Yet, it also ignited a renewed resolve, planting the seeds for future battles and keeping alive the enduring spirit of the fight for gender justice.

CHINA'S ECONOMIC REFORMS TAKE SHAPE

In Beijing, a quiet yet profound transformation was taking shape. Guided by Deng Xiaoping's leadership, China's Communist Party Congress adopted a new constitution in December, cementing the nation's gradual turn toward market-driven reforms. Across the countryside, a fresh spirit of enterprise emerged as the Household Responsibility System allowed farmers to retain profits from surplus crops. These sweeping changes marked the first steps of China's path from a closed economy to the global force it would one day become, leaving an enduring imprint on the fabric of the world economy.

CANADA ADOPTS A NEW CONSTITUTION

April 17 was a proud day of celebration in Canada, as Queen Elizabeth II personally signed the Constitution Act into law. This historic moment brought Canada's constitution home from the United Kingdom, granting the nation full sovereignty. The act also introduced the Canadian Charter of Rights and Freedoms, a document that has since become a defining pillar of Canadian identity. For many Canadians, this day represented more than a political achievement—it stood as a heartfelt declaration of the nation's coming of age.

THE GREENHAM COMMON PEACE CAMP

In a quiet Berkshire field, a powerful movement was quietly taking root. Women from across the United Kingdom gathered at Greenham Common to protest the stationing of nuclear missiles at the airbase. The peace camp grew into a symbol of grassroots defiance, its modest tents and hand-painted signs standing in sharp contrast to the looming threat of nuclear war. Their enduring chant—"Take the toys from the boys"—became both a rallying cry and a lasting reminder of the strength found in peaceful resistance.

THE DEATH OF LEONID BREZHNE

November marked the close of an era as Leonid Brezhnev, the long-standing leader of the Soviet Union, passed away. For 18 years, Brezhnev had stood at the helm, guiding a nation weighed down by stagnation and decline. His death signaled the start of a new chapter in Soviet leadership, a quiet prelude to the sweeping and dramatic transformations that would shape the course of the decade ahead.

THE UNVEILING OF THE VIETNAM VETERANS MEMORIAL

In November, Washington, D.C., witnessed a poignant moment of healing as the Vietnam Veterans Memorial was unveiled. Its solemn black granite walls, engraved with the names of over 58,000 fallen soldiers, offered a sacred space for reflection and mourning. Families traced the etched names with trembling fingers, seeking fragments of closure. This memorial stood as more than a tribute; it was a quiet step toward reconciling a nation still scarred by the lingering shadows of a painful war.

GANDHI AND THE PATH OF NONVIOLENCE

On the global stage, India honored the centenary of Mahatma Gandhi's birth. His timeless philosophy of nonviolence continued to shine as a guiding light for activists across the world, from anti-apartheid efforts in South Africa to civil rights battles in the United States. The year stood as a poignant reminder of the enduring strength of Gandhi's teachings, proving that the universal call for justice and peace could transcend borders and generations alike.

ACTIVITY: BREAKING NEWS QUIZ TEST YOUR KNOWLEDGE OF 1982'S HEADLINES

Question 1: What significant conflict began on April 2, 1982, over a group of remote islands?

A) The Gulf War

B) The Falklands War

C) The Iran-Iraq War

D) The Suez Crisis

Question 2: What tragic event unfolded in the Sabra and Shatila refugee camps in September 1982?

A) A bomb explosion

B) A flood disaster

C) A massacre

D) An earthquake

Question 3: What safety innovation followed the Tylenol murders in Chicago?

   A) New product labeling

   B) Childproof caps

   C) Tamper-proof packaging

   D) Digital expiration dates

Question 4: On January 13, 1982, which tragic airline accident claimed 78 lives after plunging into the frozen Potomac River?

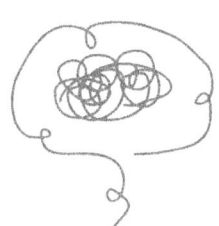

   A) Air France Flight 90

   B) Pan Am Flight 90

   C) Air Florida Flight 90

   D) Delta Airlines Flight 90

Question 5: What disaster in France claimed the lives of 46 children on July 31, 1982?

   A) Train derailment

   B) Beaune coach crash

   C) School collapse

   D) Factory explosion

Question 6: Which organization was responsible for the Hyde Park and Regent's Park bombings in London?

A) IRA

B) ETA

C) Red Army Faction

D) Baader-Meinhof Group

Question 7: Where did Pan Am Flight 759 crash shortly after takeoff in July 1982?

A) Miami, Florida

B) Kenner, Louisiana

C) Dallas, Texas

D) San Diego, California

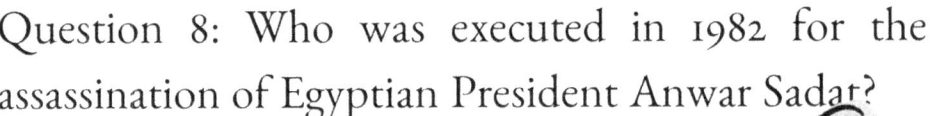

Question 8: Who was executed in 1982 for the assassination of Egyptian President Anwar Sadat?

A) Khalid Islambouli

B) Ayman al-Zawahiri

C) Osama bin Laden

D) Yasser Arafat

Question 9: Which Peruvian diplomat became the first Latin American UN Secretary-General in 1982?

A) Javier Pérez de Cuéllar
B) César Gaviria
C) Kofi Annan
D) Ban Ki-moon

Question 10: What significant feminist milestone failed to pass in the United States in 1982?

A) Roe v. Wade
B) Equal Rights Amendment
C) Voting Rights Act
D) Title IX

Question 11: What major reform allowed Chinese farmers to retain profits from surplus crops in 1982?

A) Green Revolution
B) Rural Entrepreneurship Act
C) Household Responsibility System
D) Agrarian Reforms Act

Question 12: What key event marked Canada's declaration of full sovereignty in 1982?

A) Adoption of a new flag

B) Signing of the Constitution Act

C) Opening of Parliament Hill

D) Independence from France

Question 13: What peace movement emerged in Berkshire, England, to protest nuclear missiles in 1982?

A) Green Revolution
B) Greenham Common
Peace Camp
C) Greenpeace
Activists United
D) Women Against War

Question 14: Who passed away in 1982 after leading the Soviet Union for 18 years?

A) Mikhail Gorbachev

B) Joseph Stalin

C) Leonid Brezhnev

D) Nikita Khrushchev

Question 15: What memorial was unveiled in Washington, D.C., in November 1982, honoring 58,000 fallen soldiers?

A) World War II Memorial

B) Vietnam Veterans Memorial

C) Korean War Memorial

D) Arlington National Cemetery

CHAPTER 2

HOLLYWOOD & GLOBAL CINEMA IN 1982

2.1 Iconic Films, Studios, and Actors of the Year

E.T. the Extra-Terrestrial –
A Heartwarming Tale of Friendship

It was the summer when hearts around the world learned to dream again. Steven Spielberg, already celebrated as a master of cinema, unveiled E.T. the Extra-Terrestrial, a story so tender and universal it surpassed both genre and geography. The tale of young Elliott

24

and his otherworldly companion, E.T., became a hymn to childhood wonder and the enduring strength of friendship. When E.T. lifted Elliott's bicycle into the night sky, silhouetted by the glowing moon, audiences collectively gasped. Who didn't shed tears when E.T. raised his glowing finger and softly promised, "I'll be right here"? With John Williams' magical score soaring through theaters, E.T. transformed into more than a film—it became a cultural phenomenon that left millions both tearful and inspired.

Blade Runner – A Dystopian Future Masterpiece

In stark contrast to Spielberg's heartfelt masterpiece, Ridley Scott unveiled a shadowed vision of the future with Blade Runner. The rain-slicked, neon-lit streets of 2019 Los Angeles became the haunting backdrop for this dystopian exploration of replicants and morality. Harrison Ford's portrayal of Rick Deckard captured the weary essence of an antihero, searching for meaning as much as fugitives. Rutger Hauer's mesmerizing performance as Roy Batty elevated the film's soul, culminating in the immortal line, "All those moments will be lost in time, like tears in rain." Misunderstood upon its release, Blade Runner slowly evolved into a cult classic, celebrated for its meditative depth, breathtaking visual design, and the timeless questions it dares to ask about humanity itself.

Gandhi – A Monumental Historical Epic

Meanwhile, across the Atlantic, director Richard Attenborough was shaping an epic that would forever redefine biographical cinema. Gandhi brought the life of Mahatma Gandhi to the screen with breathtaking authenticity. Ben Kingsley's transformative portrayal was so profound that many viewers felt they were watching the true Gandhi himself. From the salt marches to his quiet acts of resistance, the film captured the spirit of a man who reshaped history through nonviolence. It was far more than a historical drama; it became a global lesson on the timeless strength of peace. Gandhi swept the Academy Awards, including Best Picture, leaving an enduring imprint on both world cinema and humanity's collective memory.

The Thing –
Paranoia in the Frozen Wilderness

In the frozen desolation of Antarctica, John Carpenter delivered a chilling masterpiece of paranoia and fear with The Thing. Its shape-shifting alien and groundbreaking practical effects made the film an unrelenting, visceral experience. Kurt Russell's portrayal of the rugged, reluctant hero R.J. MacReady added weight to a harrowing tale of mistrust and survival. Though critics initially met its bleak tone with indifference, The Thing later rose to claim its place as a defining pillar of horror, celebrated for its psychological depth and the nerve-wracking tension that still grips audiences.

Tootsie – Comedy with a Purpose

Dustin Hoffman captivated audiences in Tootsie, a comedy brimming with heart and meaning. As Michael Dorsey, an actor so desperate for work that he disguises himself as a woman, Hoffman delivered one of the most remarkable performances of his career. The film was more than a lighthearted romp; it boldly questioned societal norms and offered a clever critique of gender roles. Jessica Lange's tender yet empowering portrayal added another layer of brilliance to the story. As audiences laughed, they also paused to reflect—a timeless hallmark of storytelling at its very best.

First Blood – The Birth of an Action Hero

John Sturges' The Magnificent Seven captured the spirit of Akira Kurosawa's Seven Samurai and reimagined it against the rugged backdrop of the American West. Yul Brynner, Steve McQueen, and a stellar ensemble infused the story of hired guns defending a Mexican village from bandits with both grit and charisma. Elmer Bernstein's stirring score became forever linked with adventure, its notes echoing themes of sacrifice and camaraderie that deeply resonated with audiences. The film revitalized the Western genre, breathing new life into its traditions, and secured its enduring place within the timeless pantheon of cinematic classics.

The Man from Snowy River – A Love Letter to the Australian Outback

From the rolling hills of Australia came The Man from Snowy River, a story steeped in rugged beauty and unyielding spirit. Tom Burlinson's portrayal of Jim Craig, a young man striving to reclaim his legacy, resonated deeply with audiences. The film's sweeping cinematography and stirring score felt like a heartfelt love letter to Australia's wilderness. It remained a reminder that courage and perseverance are virtues forever timeless.

Pink Floyd – The Wall –
Music and Madness Collide

Few films have merged music and storytelling as seamlessly as Pink Floyd – The Wall. This surreal, experimental journey drew audiences into the anguished mind of a rock star spiraling into isolation. Roger Waters' haunting lyrics, paired with Alan Parker's daring direction, created a cinematic experience unlike anything before. The film's striking animation sequences, combined with its raw emotion, transformed it into a haunting masterpiece —an enduring triumph of both sight and sound.

2.2 TV Shows That Captivated the Nation

Cheers – Where Everybody Knows Your Name

In 1982, audiences were invited into a warm Boston bar where the beer flowed cold, and the conversation felt like comfort. Cheers premiered with its now-iconic theme song and an ensemble cast that instantly felt like old friends. Ted Danson's Sam Malone, the charming ex-baseball star turned bartender, exchanged quick-witted banter with Diane Chambers, the refined waitress brought to life by Shelley Long. The show's magic was its ability to make viewers feel at home, sharing laughs with lovable regulars like Norm and Cliff. With its blend of sharp humor and heartfelt moments, Cheers quickly became the place "where everybody knows your name."

Family Ties – Love and Politics in the Keaton Household

Few shows reflected the generational divide of the 1980s as poignantly as Family Ties. Michael J. Fox starred as the driven and conservative Alex P. Keaton, whose Reagan-era values clashed with the liberal ideals of his hippie parents, played by Meredith Baxter and Michael Gross. Each episode blended humor with heartfelt lessons, exploring themes of love, family, and compromise. Fox's charm and sharp comedic timing made Alex an iconic character, while Family Ties became a beloved Thursday night staple, resonating with audiences navigating the shifting values of the decade.

Knight Rider – A Man and His Car Against the World

In 1982, Knight Rider roared onto television screens with action, intrigue, and a talking car. David Hasselhoff portrayed Michael Knight, a crime-fighter with a shadowy past and a futuristic partner —KITT, a sleek, intelligent Pontiac Trans Am voiced by William Daniels. The show blended cutting-edge technology with timeless heroics, turning each episode into a pulse-pounding adventure. For kids and adults alike, Knight Rider was more than just entertainment; it was a symbol of effortless cool, a thrilling fantasy where justice and courage always seemed destined to prevail.

St. Elsewhere – Breaking New Ground in Medical Drama

Before Grey's Anatomy or ER, there was St. Elsewhere, the gritty, groundbreaking medical drama that premiered in 1982. Set within the fictional St. Eligius Hospital, the series followed an ensemble cast of doctors, nurses, and patients, capturing both the triumphs and tragedies that defined life in the medical field. With its raw storytelling and layered characters, St. Elsewhere broke away from polished, sanitized depictions of hospitals, offering a more authentic and often sobering view of healthcare. The show became a critical favorite, paving the way for future dramas that embraced depth, realism, and emotional complexity.

Silver Spoons – A Millionaire Kid's Dream

What child didn't dream of living in a mansion with a train rolling through the living room? Silver Spoons made that fantasy real, following Ricky Stratton, a boy reconnecting with his eccentric, toy-loving millionaire father. Starring Ricky Schroder and Joel Higgins, the show blended comedy with heartfelt moments, exploring themes of family, forgiveness, and growing up. For kids of the 1980s, Silver Spoons was more than entertainment—it was a weekly escape filled with warmth, laughter, and the charm of childhood dreams.

Hill Street Blues – Life on the Streets

In a television landscape filled with formulaic police dramas, Hill Street Blues stood as a revelation. Premiering a year earlier, the show found its stride in 1982, delivering a gritty, character-driven portrait of life within an urban police precinct. Its layered storytelling and morally complex characters, from Captain Frank Furillo to the unpredictable Detective Mick Belker, redefined what TV drama could be. With its somber opening theme and unflinching realism, Hill Street Blues became more than a show—it offered viewers an emotional journey into the human struggles behind the badge.

Three's Company – Hijinks in Apartment 201

By 1982, Three's Company was already a cultural phenomenon, delighting audiences with its zany misunderstandings and beloved characters. John Ritter's Jack Tripper, pretending to be gay to share an apartment with two women, delivered a comedic performance of pure brilliance. The antics of roommates Janet and Terri, along with nosy landlord Mr. Furley, turned every episode into laughter. Though light and silly, the show's true magic was its ability to bring joy, warmth, and escapism to millions of viewers weekly.

Magnum, P.I. – Paradise and Private Investigations

In Magnum, P.I., Tom Selleck's charismatic portrayal of Thomas Magnum, a laid-back private investigator in sun-soaked Hawaii, was nothing short of iconic. With his trademark mustache, vibrant Hawaiian shirts, and sleek red Ferrari, Magnum embodied the essence of 1980s cool. The show's mix of action, humor, and heartfelt moments resonated deeply, making Magnum a beloved character whose style and charm continue to inspire nostalgia decades later.

The Love Boat – Romance on the High Seas

Sailing into another successful season, The Love Boat in 1982 remained a Saturday night favorite. Each week, Captain Stubing and his crew welcomed guest stars aboard their luxury cruise ship, where romance, laughter, and occasional drama unfolded beneath the ocean skies. The show's comforting formula made it a family favorite, while its glamorous setting offered a dreamy glimpse into an aspirational world of adventure and love.

ACTIVITY: 1982 CINEMA AND TELEVISION CHALLENGE

Question 1: Which 1982 film featured a young boy forming a heartfelt bond with an alien who wanted to "phone home"?

    A) Close Encounters of the Third Kind

    B) E.T. the Extra-Terrestrial

    C) The Last Starfighter

    D) Starman

Question 2: In Blade Runner, what is Rick Deckard's primary role in the dystopian future of 2019 Los Angeles?

    A) He's a replicant designer

    B) He's a replicant hunter

    C) He's a spaceship pilot

    D) He's a time traveler

Question 3: Which historical epic won eight Academy Awards in 1982, including Best Picture?

    A) Chariots of Fire

    B) Gandhi

    C) The Mission

    D) Out of Africa

Question 4: What is the setting of the horror masterpiece The Thing, directed by John Carpenter?

A) An isolated Antarctic research station

B) A haunted suburban home

C) A derelict spaceship

D) A New York City hospital

Question 5: In Tootsie, what does Dustin Hoffman's character do to land a role in a soap opera?

A) Pretends to be a doctor

B) Pretends to be a woman

C) Pretends to be British

D) Pretends to be a chef

Question 6: What luxurious car was the sidekick in the TV show Knight Rider?

A) A Ford Mustang

B) A Pontiac Trans Am

C) A Chevrolet Corvette

D) A DeLorean

Question 7: Which TV show introduced audiences to the hilarious antics of a Boston bar "where everybody knows your name"?

A) Taxi

B) Cheers

C) The Mary Tyler Moore Show

D) Laverne & Shirley

Question 8: What groundbreaking medical drama premiered in 1982, offering a realistic look at life in a hospital?

A) St. Elsewhere

B) General Hospital

C) MASH*

D) ER

Question 9: Which animated children's show that debuted in 1982 featured Fraggles, Doozers, and Gorgs?

A) The Muppet Show

B) Fraggle Rock

C) Sesame Street

D) Thundercats

Question 10: In the police drama Hill Street Blues, what was the theme of its opening sequence?

A) An intense car chase

B) The somber lives of officers

C) A melancholic piano tune

D) A courtroom verdict

CHAPTER 3

THE SOUND OF 1982

3.1 TOP MUSICAL HITS AND INFLUENTIAL ARTISTS ACROSS CONTINENTS

Eye of the Tiger" – Survivor: An Anthem of Resilience

If there was ever a song that made you feel ready to conquer the world, it was Survivor's Eye of the Tiger. Written for Rocky III, this adrenaline-charged anthem roared through radios across the globe, inspiring millions to rise and face their own battles. Its iconic guitar riff became the anthem of underdogs everywhere, proving that with sheer determination, anything was within reach. Even today, it's impossible to hear this track without feeling an unstoppable surge of confidence and that enduring sense of being utterly invincible.

"Ebony and Ivory" – Paul McCartney and Stevie Wonder: A Call for Harmony

When Paul McCartney and Stevie Wonder united for Ebony and Ivory, the result was a heartfelt call for racial harmony. This soulful duet topped charts worldwide, blending McCartney's melodic warmth with Wonder's unmistakable voice. The piano metaphor—black and white keys creating harmony —resonated deeply in a world longing for unity. It wasn't just a song; it was a timeless message of hope and togetherness.

"Come On Eileen" & The Folk-Pop Revolutionaries – Dexys Midnight Runners: A Joyous Celebration

The streets pulsed with the irresistible energy of Come On Eileen. With its Celtic-inspired melody and playful charm, this track had people dancing in pubs and parties from Dublin to Detroit. Dexys Midnight Runners perfectly captured the spirit of youthful exuberance, creating a song that felt like a joyous celebration of life itself. Its unforgettable refrain, "Too-ra-loo-ra-too-ra-loo-rye-ay," continues to echo in the hearts of fans, carrying with it memories of carefree nights and timeless revelry.

With their hit Come On Eileen, Dexys Midnight Runners brought a unique fusion of folk and pop to 1982. The band's unconventional style and energy made them one of the year's most distinctive acts. Their ability to merge genres and craft a song of pure celebration set them apart, leaving a lasting mark on the music of the 1980s.

"Africa" – Toto: A Song That Spanned the Globe

There's something timeless about Africa. Toto's hauntingly beautiful song, with its evocative lyrics and soaring chorus, carried listeners on a journey to a faraway continent. Its seamless blend of rock and world music elements was ahead of its era, creating a soundscape both intimate and expansive. It wasn't merely a hit—it became a global anthem that still enchants new generations.

"1999" – Prince: A Funk
Fueled Party for the Ages

Prince invited the world to celebrate like it was the end of the century with 1999. This funk-charged anthem burst with energy, merging rock, pop, and soul in a way only Prince could. It was far more than a song—it became a movement, a joyous tribute to life and music amid uncertainty. Prince's flamboyant style and fearless creativity turned 1999 into an instant classic that continues to define an era of bold expression and unforgettable sound.

"The Message" – Grandmaster Flash and the Furious Five: Hip-Hop's Awakening

In 1982, hip-hop found its true voice with The Message. Grandmaster Flash and the Furious Five painted a striking portrait of urban life, blending sharp lyrics with a gripping beat. The song's raw honesty about social issues was groundbreaking, shifting from party anthems to a genre of powerful commentary. The Message wasn't just music; it became a movement, shaping socially conscious rap.

3.2 Influential Figures Shaping the Music Industry Domestically and Internationally

Michael Jackson

The King Takes the Throne

If any name defined 1982, it was Michael Jackson. The release of Thriller in late November didn't just make waves—it created a cultural tsunami felt across the globe. Jackson's masterful fusion of pop, R&B, and funk reshaped the genre, while his magnetic stage presence made him a worldwide phenomenon. From the unforgettable "Billie Jean" bassline to the eerie rhythms of Thriller, Jackson didn't just craft music; he wrote

His music videos, cinematic in scope, shattered barriers on MTV, while his dazzling moonwalk and sequined glove became enduring icons of superstardom. In 1982, Michael Jackson wasn't simply an artist—he was a revolution.

Quincy Jones – The Visionary Producer

Behind the magic of Thriller stood Quincy Jones, a producer with a golden touch. Already a legendary figure, Jones infused his deep knowledge of jazz, pop, and orchestration into Jackson's music, crafting a sound both groundbreaking and timeless. His meticulous attention to detail and gift for blending influences made Thriller the best-selling album ever. Jones wasn't just shaping music; he was creating a blueprint for excellence that continues to inspire generations of producers and artists.

Prince – The Purple One's Reign Begins

While Michael Jackson ruled pop, Prince was forging his own path as the enigmatic genius of funk and rock. His 1982 hit 1999 became an anthem for the ages, mixing infectious rhythms with a playful yet apocalyptic message. Prince's ability to effortlessly blend genres, from funk to rock to new wave, made him a true trailblazer. His flamboyant style, fearless creativity, and mastery of multiple instruments elevated him to an almost mythical status. By the close of 1982, Prince wasn't simply an artist—he was an icon in the making.

Madonna – A Star on the Rise

1982 marked the dawn of Madonna's rise to superstardom. With her debut single "Everybody," she boldly introduced herself to the world as a fearless and unapologetic performer. Madonna's distinctive mix of pop, dance, and attitude set her apart, while her remarkable control over both image and sound revealed a business savvy rarely seen in the industry. Though only at the beginning of her journey, it was clear that Madonna was destined to become far more than a pop star—she was on the path to becoming a cultural icon.

Grandmaster Flash – The Voice of Hip-Hop's Awakening

In 1982, hip-hop made a bold stride toward mainstream recognition, led by Grandmaster Flash and the Furious Five. Their groundbreaking track The Message delivered a raw, unflinching portrayal of life in the inner city, pairing rhythmic beats with lyrics that carried sharp social awareness. Flash's pioneering mastery of turntables and his ability to craft intricate soundscapes elevated hip-hop from party music to a genre capable of profound storytelling. In a year overflowing with hits, The Message rose above the rest, declaring that hip-hop had arrived—and had something powerful and important to say.

Joan Jett – The Rebel Queen of Rock

Joan Jett was unstoppable in 1982, shattering barriers and stereotypes with her explosive hit I Love Rock 'n' Roll. As a woman thriving in a male-dominated rock scene, Jett's success was nothing short of groundbreaking. Her no-nonsense attitude, gritty vocals, and electrifying stage presence made her a beacon of empowerment for women everywhere. Jett didn't just sing about loving rock; she lived it, becoming a fearless trailblazer who paved the way for countless future generations of female rockers.

Paul McCartney – A Living Legend

Even after decades in the spotlight, Paul McCartney continued shaping music in 1982. His duet with Stevie Wonder on Ebony and Ivory was a heartfelt plea for unity that resonated across continents. The former Beatle proved his gift for crafting timeless melodies and forging deep connections with audiences remained as powerful as ever. McCartney's influence in 1982 served as a reminder that genuine artistry, once ignited, carries an enduring light that knows no boundaries or expiration date.

Stevie Wonder – The Soulful Trailblazer

By 1982, Stevie Wonder was already a music legend, but his collaboration with Paul McCartney on Ebony and Ivory solidified his standing as a global force for good. Wonder's rare gift for merging soul, pop, and activism made him a beacon of hope. His music transcended boundaries, delivering messages of love, peace, and resilience the world deeply needed.

Toto – Masters of Melody

While some artists ruled through showmanship, Toto quietly captivated the world with their unmatched musical craftsmanship. Their 1982 hit Africa became a global phenomenon, weaving intricate harmonies with rich, worldly influences. Toto's meticulous production and gift for creating songs that struck deep emotional chords made them a standout act in what was already an extraordinary and unforgettable year for music.

ACTIVITY: 1982 MUSIC MASHUP – GUESS THE SONG OR ARTIST

Test your knowledge of the unforgettable tracks and influential figures of 1982! Match the correct answer to each clue. These questions celebrate the hits and legends that defined the sound of a generation.

Question 1: Which iconic song by Survivor became an anthem for underdogs after being featured in Rocky III?

A) Burning Heart

B) Eye of the Tiger

C) Danger Zone

D) The Final Countdown

Question 2: Paul McCartney and Stevie Wonder collaborated on a chart-topping hit in 1982. What was the song's name?

A) Ebony and Ivory   C) We Are the World

B) Say Say Say   D) Endless Love

Question 3: Which song by Dexys Midnight Runners had everyone singing "Too-ra-loo-ra-too-ra-loo-rye-ay"?

A) Come On Eileen

B) The Safety Dance

C) Tainted Love

D) Don't You Want Me

Question 4: Toto's Africa is one of the most beloved songs from 1982. What element of the song made it stand out?

A) Its futuristic sound effects

B) Its fusion of rock and world music elements

C) Its all-instrumental nature

D) Its focus on political issues

Question 5: Which artist released the funk-fueled anthem 1999, celebrating life in the face of uncertainty?

A) Michael Jackson
B) Prince
C) Lionel Richie
D) Bruce Springsteen

Question 6: Grandmaster Flash and the Furious Five made waves in 1982 with a song highlighting urban life's struggles. What was it called?

A) The Breaks
B) Rapper's Delight
C) The Message
D) Planet Rock

Question 7: Michael Jackson's Thriller was released in 1982. Which song from the album features the unforgettable bassline?

A) Thriller
B) Billie Jean
C) Beat It
D) Wanna Be Startin' Somethin'

Question 8: Joan Jett's empowering rock anthem became a symbol of rebellion in 1982. What was the song?

A) Hit Me with Your Best Shot

B) I Love Rock 'n' Roll

C) Barracuda

D) Edge of Seventeen

Question 9: Which iconic song by Toto became a global phenomenon for its intricate harmonies and emotional resonance?

A) Hold the Line

B) Rosanna

C) Africa

D) Don't Stop Believin'

Question 10: Which artist released their debut single Everybody in 1982, marking the beginning of an ascent to superstardom?

A) Whitney Houston   C) Madonna

B) Cyndi Lauper   D) Janet Jackson

CHAPTER 4

SPORTS IN 1982: HISTORIC WINS AND MEMORABLE MOMENTS

World-Class Sporting Events: Athletic Achievements and Memorable Victories

January 2, 1982: "The Epic in Miami"
A Game for the Ages

The sweltering heat of Miami set the stage for one of the greatest and most unforgettable games in NFL history. On January 2, the San Diego Chargers faced the Miami Dolphins in an AFC Divisional Playoff epic forever etched in football lore. The game was an emotional rollercoaster, packed with record-breaking plays, breathtaking moments, and a dramatic overtime finale. The Chargers' 41-38 triumph wasn't just a victory—it was a powerful testament to grit, endurance, and the timeless thrill of the sport. Fans still vividly recall Kellen Winslow's heroic effort, fighting exhaustion and injury, blocking a pivotal field goal, and amassing an incredible 166 receiving yards.

January 10, 1982: "The Catch"
A Moment of Perfection

Candlestick Park crackled with energy as the San Francisco 49ers battled the Dallas Cowboys in the NFC Championship. With only 58 seconds left, Joe Montana rolled out under relentless pressure and floated a pass to Dwight Clark in the end zone. Clark's soaring fingertip catch, forever remembered as "The Catch," sealed the 49ers' 28-27 victory and their path to the Super Bowl. The moment was more than a game-winner—it became an enduring symbol of the 49ers' rise to greatness and one of the most iconic, artistic plays in NFL history.

January 24, 1982: Super Bowl XVI
The 49ers' First Glory

Two weeks later, the 49ers capped their Cinderella season by defeating the Cincinnati Bengals 26-21 in Super Bowl XVI. Played at the Pontiac Silverdome in Michigan, the game showcased Joe Montana's remarkable poise and leadership. With pinpoint passing and an unshakable calm under pressure, Montana guided his team to their first-ever Super Bowl triumph, earning MVP honors. For the 49ers and their devoted fans, it marked the dawn of a new era, as the team firmly cemented its place among the NFL's most celebrated and enduring dynasties.

June 13 – July 11, 1982: Italy's Glory at the FIFA World Cup

The world's attention turned to Spain as it hosted the 1982 FIFA World Cup, a tournament bursting with drama, skill, and unforgettable moments. Italy's path to victory was nothing short of miraculous. Led by striker Paolo Rossi, the tournament's top scorer, Italy defeated Argentina, Brazil, and West Germany in a breathtaking run. In the July 11 final, Italy triumphed 3-1 over West Germany, claiming their third World Cup title. Rossi's six goals and redemption arc after a ban made him a national hero, uniting a jubilant Italy.

July 7, 1982:

Jimmy Connors Triumphs at Wimbledon

On Wimbledon's famed grass courts, American tennis star Jimmy Connors earned a career-defining triumph. Facing rival John McEnroe in the final, Connors fought through a mid-match slump to win in five thrilling sets (3-6, 6-3, 6-7, 7-6, 6-4). The match highlighted Connors' resilience and fiery spirit, securing his second Wimbledon singles title. It was a comeback story that resonated deeply with fans, proving that grit and determination could conquer even the fiercest challenges.

July 10, 1982: Martina Navratilova's Wimbledon Dominance

Just days after Connors' triumph, Martina Navratilova added another chapter to her Wimbledon legacy. In the women's singles final, Navratilova overpowered her fierce rival Chris Evert-Lloyd with a commanding performance (6-1, 3-6, 6-2). The victory marked her third Wimbledon singles title, cementing her place among the greatest players in tennis history. Navratilova's unmatched blend of power and precision, combined with her storied rivalry with Evert, remained a treasured gift for tennis fans around the world.

September 11, 1982:

Connors' Fifth US Open Victory

Jimmy Connors returned to the spotlight later that year at the US Open, capturing his fifth singles title. Facing the formidable Ivan Lendl in the final, Connors displayed his trademark determination and triumphed in four sets (6-3, 6-2, 4-6, 6-4). The victory was a testament to Connors' ability to thrive under pressure and his lasting place at the pinnacle of men's tennis. The crowd at Flushing Meadows roared in approval, celebrating one of the sport's most enduring icons.

September 12, 1982:
Chris Evert's Sixth US Open Title

Chris Evert extended her dominance in women's tennis by winning her sixth US Open singles title, defeating Hana Mandlíková in straight sets. Evert's grace on the court and unmatched consistency made her a beloved favorite. Her victory at Flushing Meadows was yet another reminder of her enduring brilliance, further cementing her legacy as one of the greatest athletes in the history of tennis.

October 20, 1982:

St. Louis Cardinals Win the World Series

The fall delivered baseball's grand finale, as the St. Louis Cardinals faced the Milwaukee Brewers in a thrilling World Series. The Cardinals captured the championship in Game 7 with a 6-3 victory, fueled by clutch hitting and stellar pitching. The win marked their ninth World Series title, and for fans, it was a moment of pride and joy. The 1982 World Series remains among the most exciting in baseball history, a testament to the drama and unpredictability that define the sport.

November 9, 1982:
Sugar Ray Leonard's First Farewell

In a stunning announcement, boxing legend Sugar Ray Leonard retired at just 26, citing a detached retina. Leonard's departure sent shockwaves through the boxing world, as he was at the peak of his career. Known for his dazzling speed, footwork, and charisma, Leonard had already secured legendary status. Though it wouldn't be his final farewell, his 1982 retirement marked the close of a brilliant chapter in the sport's history, leaving fans both stunned and nostalgic.

ACTIVITY: SPORTS HISTORY PUZZLE – MATCH THE EVENT WITH THE YEAR'S GREATEST WINS

Match the following sports stars or teams to their most notable 1982 achievement. See if you can pair each sporting hero or event with their moment of triumph from that exciting year!

Sports Events:
1. San Diego Chargers
2. Joe Montana
3. Italy's National Soccer Team
4. Martina Navratilova
5. Jimmy Connors
6. St. Louis Cardinals
7. Sugar Ray Leonard
8. Chris Evert
9. Dwight Clark
10. Paolo Ross

Achievements:

A) Won their ninth World Series title by defeating the Milwaukee Brewers in Game 7.

B) Led his team to their first Super Bowl victory and was named MVP of the game.

C) Captured her sixth US Open singles title with a commanding performance.

D) Became a national hero after scoring six goals and leading his team to their third FIFA World Cup title.

E) Played through exhaustion and injury, delivering a heroic performance in "The Epic in Miami."

F) Retired from professional boxing at the age of 26, citing a detached retina.

G) Secured her third Wimbledon singles title by defeating her fierce rival Chris Evert.

H) Made "The Catch," a legendary fingertip grab that secured his team's place in the Super Bowl.

I) Defeated John McEnroe in a five-set thriller to claim his second Wimbledon singles title.

J) Scored the decisive goals for his team, leading them to victories over Brazil, Argentina, and West Germany.

CHAPTER 5

FASHION AND POP CULTURE IN 1982

The Rise of Power Dressing – Authority in Every Stitch

As women rose to more prominent roles in the corporate world, their fashion mirrored their ambition. Power dressing became the ultimate statement: "I mean business." Picture broad-shouldered blazers, cinched waists, and tailored suits radiating authority. Designers like Giorgio Armani led the movement, crafting sharp, minimalist silhouettes that defined the era. It wasn't just about style—it was about earning respect. Women entered boardrooms with unshakable confidence, proudly wearing their success on their sleeves—both figuratively and, in this bold fashion era, quite literally.

Neon Dreams – Colors That Dared to Be Loud

If there was one thing 1982 embraced without hesitation, it was color. Neon hues lit up the fashion world, from electric pinks and fiery oranges to lime greens and blazing yellows. These daring shades weren't confined to the dance floor—they adorned jackets, dresses, tights, and even leg warmers. Strolling down a street in 1982 felt like stepping into a living rainbow, with every outfit crafted to demand attention. Neon fashion was never just a fleeting trend; it stood as a bold declaration that life was meant to be celebrated, experienced, and lived unapologetically in dazzling, unapologetic color.

Denim Takes the Spotlight – Acid-Wash and Designer Jeans

Denim in 1982 was far from ordinary blue jeans. Acid-wash styles, with their bleached and marbled patterns, became the ultimate statement piece. Whether paired with cropped tops or oversized sweaters, they radiated cool rebellion. Designer jeans from brands like Calvin Klein and Jordache elevated denim from casual wear to high fashion. Ads with sultry taglines like "Nothing comes between me and my Calvins" turned jeans into coveted status symbols. Denim had never looked— or felt—so unapologetically chic and iconic.

Parachute Pants – The Street Style Revolution

The street style of 1982 witnessed the unstoppable rise of parachute pants. Crafted from lightweight nylon with a baggy, futuristic flair, these pants became the uniform of breakdancers and hip-hop enthusiasts alike. They weren't just designed for movement; they carried a cultural message of individuality and rebellion. Pair them with a bold graphic tee, high-top sneakers, and a bucket hat, and you had the quintessential urban look. Parachute pants seamlessly blurred the boundary between fashion and function, laying the groundwork for streetwear's lasting influence and dominance in the years that followed.

Fitness Meets Fashion – Leg Warmers and Leotards
The fitness craze of the early '80s transformed more than workout habits—it reshaped fashion itself. Fueled by Jane Fonda's workout videos, athletic wear became everyday attire. Leg warmers, leotards, and spandex leggings were no longer limited to the gym. Instead, they hit the streets, paired with oversized sweatshirts or layered under skirts. This vibrant athleisure trend infused wardrobes with energy and playfulness, proving that looking good and feeling good could truly go hand in hand.

The Power of Accessories – Bigger, Brighter, Bolder Accessories in 1982 were all about bold statements. Oversized earrings swung dramatically, chunky necklaces gleamed with rhinestones, and wide belts cinched waists with flair. Costume jewelry was unapologetically vibrant, with plastic bangles in every color of the rainbow stacked high on wrists. Even sunglasses got an upgrade, boasting bold hues and quirky shapes. No outfit felt complete without a hint of over-the-top glam, turning ordinary days into something that felt like a celebration.

Jelly Shoes – A Quirky Footwear Fad

One of the quirkiest fashion trends of 1982 was the rise of jelly shoes. Crafted from colorful PVC plastic, these translucent shoes were as fun as they were practical. Affordable and offered in a rainbow of shades, jelly shoes became a favorite among both kids and adults. Whether worn to the beach or paired with casual dresses, these playful shoes added a nostalgic touch of whimsy to the year's fashion landscape.

Runways Go Avant-Garde
Designers Push Boundaries

The high-fashion runways of 1982 overflowed with drama and daring experimentation. Designers like Jean-Paul Gaultier and Thierry Mugler embraced bold, avant-garde styles, reshaping ideas of what fashion could be. Picture asymmetrical cuts, metallic fabrics, and futuristic silhouettes that looked more like art than clothing. Eveningwear sparkled with sequins, satins, and dramatic ruffles, proving glamour was here to stay. The runways of 1982 weren't merely showcases—they were unforgettable spectacles of creativity and extravagance.

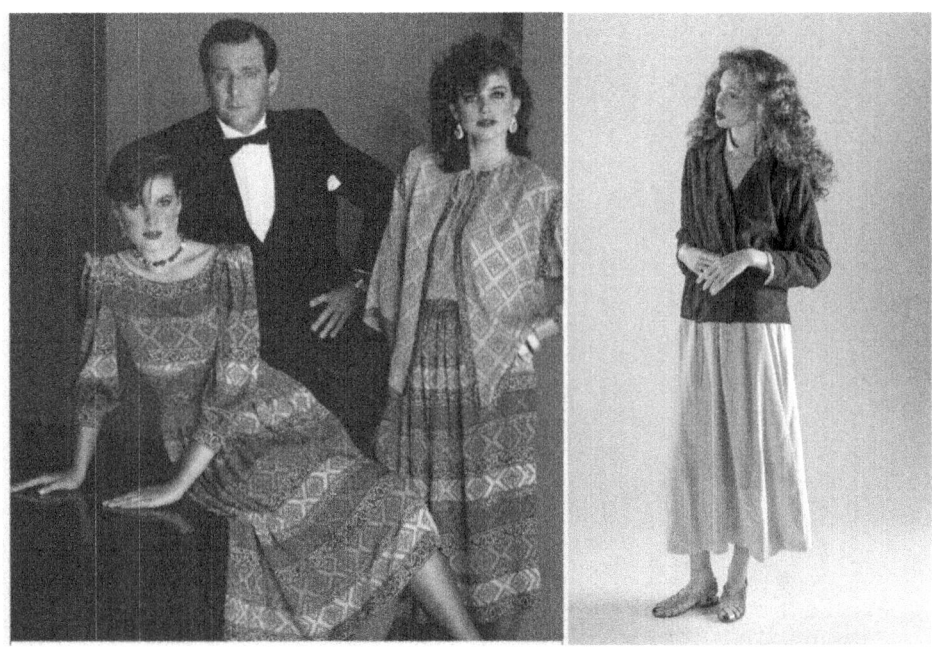

Hair and Makeup – A Celebration of Excess

Fashion in 1982 didn't stop at clothing—it extended to hair and makeup. Hairstyles reached new heights with teased bangs, voluminous curls, and blowouts that seemed to defy gravity. Makeup followed suit, featuring bold blue eyeshadow, bright blush, and glossy lips for a look that was unapologetically daring. Neon nail polish added the finishing touch, ensuring every detail of the 1982 style was vibrant, unforgettable, and full of fearless personality.

FASHION MEMORY QUIZ
RELIVE THE TRENDS OF 1982

Now that you've learned about the fashionable trends of 1982, let's test your memory! In this quiz, you'll revisit the styles, materials, and accessories that defined the era. See how many details you can recall from this chapter and relive the glamour of the 1980s through fashion.

Instructions: Circle the correct answer for each question based on the chapter. Once you've completed the quiz, check the answers to see how well you remembered the key fashion trends of 1982.

Question 1: What was the defining feature of the "power dressing" trend that became popular in 1982?

A) Neon tights

B) Oversized, padded shoulders

C) Acid-wash jeans

D) Bell-bottom pants

Question 2: Acid-wash jeans became a must-have item in 1982. What made them unique?

A) Their metallic sheen

B) Their bleached and marbled appearance

C) Their bell-bottom design

D) Their sequins and embroidery

Question 3: Which type of pants, made popular in 1982, were associated with breakdancers and streetwear?

A) Bell-bottoms

B) Parachute pants

C) Capri pants

D) Cargo pants

Question 4: Jane Fonda's workout videos inspired which fashion trend in 1982?

A) Tailored suits

B) Leg warmers and leotards

C) Jelly shoes

D) Turtleneck sweaters

Question 5: Oversized earrings and bold plastic bangles became iconic accessories in 1982. What was their primary appeal?

A) Subtlety

B) Vibrancy and drama

C) Minimalism

D) Sustainability

Question 6: What type of footwear, made of translucent PVC plastic, became a quirky fad in 1982?

A) Platform heels

B) Jelly shoes

C) Cowboy boots

D) Canvas sneakers

Question 7: Neon colors were a major trend in 1982. Which statement best describes their use?

A) They were reserved for evening wear.

B) They dominated everything from clothing to accessories.

C) They were used primarily in haute couture.

D) They were considered too daring for mainstream fashion.

Question 8: Designer jeans, like those by Calvin Klein, became status symbols in 1982. What tagline made Calvin Klein's ads famous?

A) "Live Boldly in Denim."

B) "Nothing comes between me and my Calvins."

C) "Designed for Your Best Fit."

D) "Forever in Blue Jeans."

Question 9: The avant-garde fashion of 1982, led by designers like Jean-Paul Gaultier, often featured what kind of silhouettes?

A) Boxy and oversized

B) Futuristic and asymmetrical

C) Flowing and bohemian

D) Structured and Victorian

Question 10: Which hairstyle trend dominated 1982?

A) Sleek and straight styles

B) Voluminous, teased hair with bangs

C) Short pixie cuts

D) Long braids

Question 11: Which makeup trend was synonymous with 1982 fashion?

A) Natural and muted tones

B) Bold blue eyeshadow and bright blush

C) Heavy eyeliner and dark lipstick

D) Glossy lips and gold accents

Question 12: What was the inspiration behind the revival of 1950s-style Capri pants in 1982?

A) Nostalgia for simpler times

B) High-fashion runway trends

C) Practicality and comfort

D) Influences from European cinema

Question 13: The fitness boom of 1982 led to which trend becoming part of streetwear?

A) Tracksuits with stripes

B) Spandex leggings paired with sweatshirts

C) Running shoes with velcro straps

D) Racerback tank tops

Question 14: Why were jelly shoes especially popular in 1982?

A) They were waterproof, colorful, and affordable.

B) They were endorsed by celebrities.

C) They came with matching handbags.

D) They were a limited-edition item.

CHAPTER 6

INNOVATIONS, AUTOMOBILES, AND TECHNOLOGY OF 1982

6.1 REVOLUTIONARY INVENTIONS AND BREAKTHROUGHS IN SCIENCE (1982)

A Lunar Meteorite Found on Earth – A Piece of the Moon in Our Hands

In Antarctica's frozen Allan Hills, scientists uncovered a discovery straight from science fiction. A lunar meteorite, later named Allan Hills A81005, lay quietly embedded within the stark, icy landscape.It was the first time humanity held a piece of the Moon that had traveled to Earth on its own, launched from the lunar surface millions of years ago.

This January 1982 discovery thrilled scientists and reignited humanity's enduring wonder about the universe.

The Rare Alignment of All Nine Planets
A Cosmic Dance

On March 10, 1982, stargazers and scientists marveled at a celestial event called a syzygy, when all nine planets in our solar system aligned on the same side of the Sun. Though invisible to the naked eye, the event stirred curiosity and awe, highlighting the vast, intricate dance of the cosmos. Some feared it would trigger seismic disasters on Earth, though science quickly dismissed such myths. Instead, the alignment reminded humanity of its small yet meaningful place in the grand design of the universe.

The Birth of the First Computer Virus – Elk Cloner
Before firewalls and antivirus software, there was Elk Cloner. Created by 15-year-old high school student Rich Skrenta, this harmless prank virus became the first to spread in the wild, infecting Apple II systems through floppy disks. Though it caused no real harm, Elk Cloner foreshadowed the cybersecurity challenges ahead. Its playful rhyming message, displayed on infected machines, brought unexpected humor to an era still largely innocent to the darker, more complex realities of digital technology that would soon shape the future.

'Tron' and the Rise
of Computer Animation in Cinema

On July 9, 1982, the world experienced Tron, a groundbreaking film that fused science with art. Using computer-generated imagery (CGI) on an unprecedented scale, the movie transported audiences into a digital world where programs battled for survival. Though the technology of the time limited visual possibilities, Tron became a trailblazer, inspiring a generation of filmmakers and paving the way for the seamless, visually stunning CGI landscapes we marvel at in modern cinema.

Synthetic Insulin
A Triumph for Medicine and Biotechnology

In 1982, biotechnology company Genentech and Eli Lilly made history with the creation of synthetic human insulin using recombinant DNA technology. This groundbreaking achievement offered a safer, more efficient way to treat diabetes, ushering in a new era of medicine. For millions living with diabetes, synthetic insulin wasn't merely an innovation—it was a lifeline. It stood as a powerful symbol of science's ability to transform lives and bring hope for a healthier future.

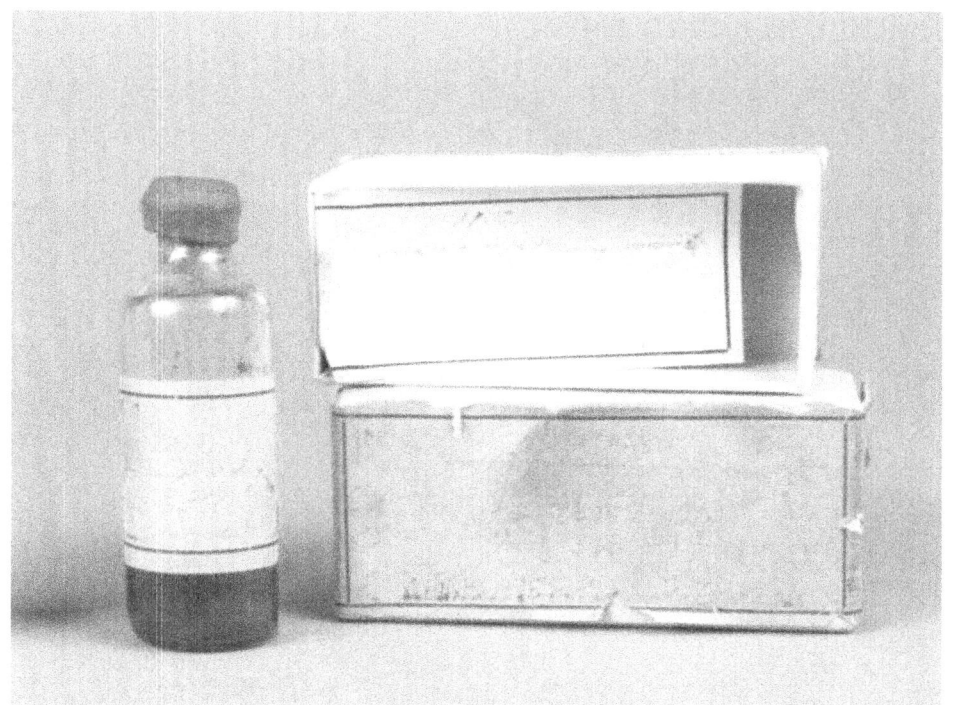

The Launch of the Sony CD Player
A New Era of Music

October 1982 marked the debut of the Sony CDP-101, the world's first commercially available compact disc player. Paired with the launch of the CD format, it revolutionized how music was experienced. For the first time, listeners could enjoy crystal-clear sound and instantly skip to favorite tracks with a button press. Gone were the frustrations of scratched vinyl and tangled cassette tapes. The CD player ushered in a golden age of digital audio, forever transforming the way the world listened to music.

Anti-Human Monoclonal Antibodies
A Medical Milestone

In September 1982, scientists marked a major breakthrough with the first production of anti-human monoclonal antibodies. These lab-engineered molecules, designed to mimic the immune system's defense against harmful pathogens, paved the way for targeted therapies treating cancer and autoimmune disorders. It was a milestone in precision medicine, offering hope for treatments carefully tailored to individual patients' unique needs.

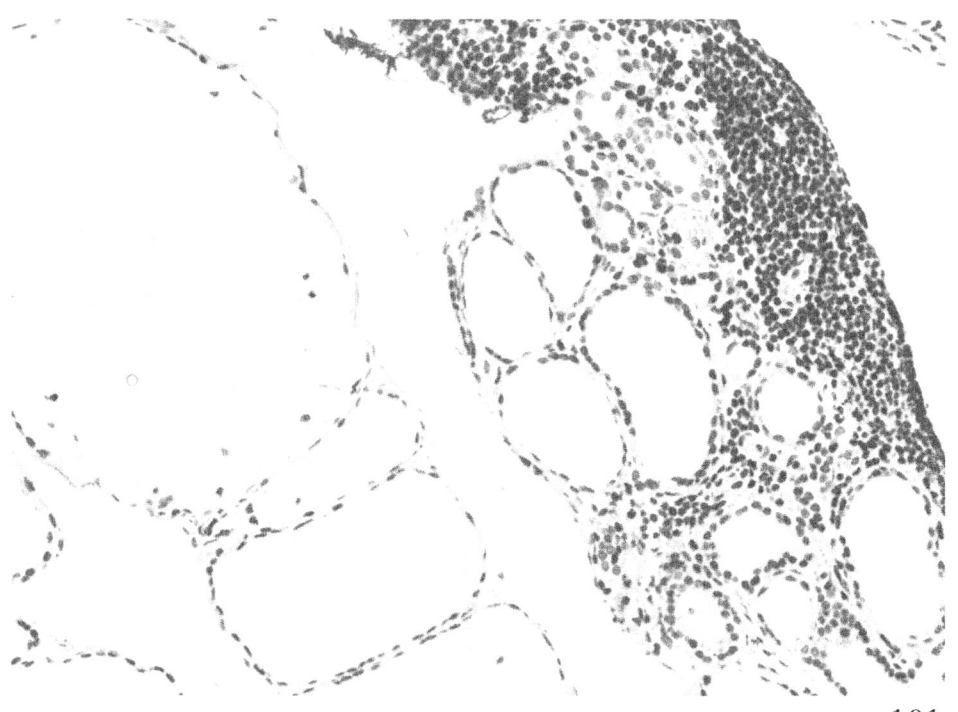

6.2 THE GOLDEN AGE OF CARS: ICONIC MODELS AND DESIGNS (1982)

The Ford Sierra: The Aerodynamic Pioneer

When Ford unveiled the Sierra in 1982, it felt like a revelation. Its streamlined design, called the "aero look," broke away from the boxy silhouettes of the previous decade. This mid-size family car blended practicality with modern style, and its aerodynamic shape wasn't just for appearance—it boosted fuel efficiency, making it a favorite in fuel-conscious Europe. For drivers, the Sierra was more than a car; it offered a thrilling glimpse into the sleek, futuristic designs shaping the automotive world ahead.

BMW 3 Series (E30): A Legend is Born

In 1982, BMW introduced the E30 generation of the 3 Series, setting a fresh benchmark for compact luxury cars. With its sharp lines, precise handling, and balance of performance and elegance, the E30 quickly became an icon. It wasn't just a car—it was a lifestyle statement. Whether cruising city streets or dominating open roads, the E30 embodied the perfect blend of sportiness and sophistication. For BMW, it marked the start of a dynasty that continues to reign supreme today.

Toyota Camry:
The Reliable Game-Changer

1982 marked the debut of the Toyota Camry, a car destined to become one of the best-selling models of all time. Celebrated for its practicality, comfort, and unwavering reliability, the Camry quickly earned a reputation as the vehicle you could trust for both everyday commutes and long road trips. It wasn't flashy, but that simplicity was its charm—it was dependable, unpretentious, and built to endure. For countless families, the Camry became more than transportation; it was a steadfast companion, and its enduring legacy continues to resonate on roads around the world today.

Porsche 944:
A Sports Car with Substance

When Porsche introduced the 944 in 1982, it was clear this wasn't just another sports car. With a front-engine, rear-wheel-drive layout and ideal 50:50 weight distribution, the 944 delivered pure driving joy. Its bold, muscular design turned heads, while its powerful engine fed the need for speed. For Porsche fans, the 944 symbolized both accessibility and performance—a sleek machine capable of conquering the track while remaining perfectly suited for everyday streets.

Nissan Micra:
Compact, Cute, and Cutting-Edge

The Nissan Micra, known as the March in some markets, debuted in 1982, ushering in a fresh era of compact cars. Small yet mighty, the Micra delivered impressive fuel efficiency and practicality within its modest frame. Its cheerful design and affordability made it a favorite among urban drivers seeking a car that was easy to park, economical, and full of charm. The Micra wasn't just transportation—it was a lifestyle statement for the fast-paced city dweller always on the move.

Mitsubishi Pajero:
The King of Off-Roading

In 1982, Mitsubishi introduced the Pajero, an SUV designed to tackle the toughest terrains with ease. With its rugged build, dependable four-wheel-drive system, and impressive durability, the Pajero quickly earned a reputation as a conqueror of mountains and deserts alike. It wasn't just for adventurers, though—its comfortable interior and versatility made it a favorite among families, too. The Pajero wasn't just an SUV; it was an invitation to explore.

Lancia Rally 037: The Rally Champion

Lancia introduced the Rally 037 in 1982, a car purpose-built to dominate rally racing. With its aggressive styling, mid-engine layout, and lightweight construction, it became a formidable force on the rally circuit. And dominate it did—the Rally 037 went on to win the 1983 World Rally Championship. For motorsport fans, the 037 wasn't just a car; it was a legend in the making, a lasting symbol of Italian engineering brilliance and unrelenting determination.

Mercedes-Benz 190 (W201):
The Baby Benz with Big Ambitions

Mercedes-Benz made waves in 1982 with the launch of the W201 series, better known as the 190. Nicknamed the "Baby Benz," it was smaller and more affordable than the brand's luxury sedans yet retained the engineering excellence Mercedes was famed for. With advanced safety features, precise handling, and a sleek design, the 190 appealed to young professionals wanting a Mercedes without breaking the bank. It became a symbol of attainable luxury, elegantly wrapped in a compact and stylish package.

Pontiac Firebird (Third Generation):
The Muscle Car Reimagined

In 1982, the Pontiac Firebird entered its third generation, and it was nothing short of a showstopper. Sleek, aerodynamic, and loaded with high-tech features like a digital dashboard, the Firebird perfectly embodied the spirit of the 1980s. It achieved even greater fame as KITT, the talking car in the hit TV show Knight Rider. For American muscle car enthusiasts, the Firebird wasn't just a vehicle—it was a cultural icon, a timeless symbol of speed, power, and undeniable cool.

Dodge 400: A Compact Contender

Rounding out 1982's lineup of iconic cars was the Dodge 400, a compact model proving practicality and style could go hand in hand. With its efficient engine, comfortable interior, and clean design, the 400 delivered an affordable yet enjoyable driving experience. It wasn't the flashiest car on the road, but its reliability and value made it stand out, winning the favor of families and budget-conscious buyers alike.

CHAPTER 7

THE COST OF LIVING IN 1982

United States – The Recession Era Reality

In 1982, America was finding its way through a recession, and every dollar seemed to stretch just a bit thinner. The median price of a new home was $82,200, a dream many worked tirelessly to afford. For renters, the average monthly cost was $320—a figure that seemed manageable but still reflected the financial strain of the time. Families filled their cars at gas stations where a gallon cost just 91 cents, a price that felt affordable yet carried echoes of the oil crises years earlier. Daily staples like a dozen eggs cost 84 cents, and a loaf of bread was 50 cents, small comforts in a challenging economy. Even amidst uncertainty, the average household income stood at $20,171, and Americans found ways to enjoy life, save for tomorrow, and dream big.

112

United Kingdom – Pint-Sized Budgets for Pint-Sized Treats

Across the Atlantic in Britain, 1982 brought a mix of affordability and austerity as the nation adjusted to its own economic shifts. The average house price stood at £33,000—a significant sum but reflective of the era's modest property values. Publicans filled pint glasses for just 61p, and breadwinners brought home loaves for 37p. Petrol cost £1.64 per gallon, a notable expense for drivers navigating Britain's winding roads. Even with these prices, the average weekly wage of £150 ensured most families could meet their needs. British culture thrived on small indulgences—milk deliveries still arrived on doorsteps at 20p a pint, and the local pub remained a warm haven where neighbors bonded over affordable ales and enduring camaraderie.

Canada – The Maple Leaf Economy

Life in Canada in 1982 was a blend of practicality and optimism. A new home cost an average of CAD 76,000, and filling up the car with gas was 34 cents per liter, making long drives across scenic landscapes affordable for many. Families found comfort in staples like a dozen eggs, priced at CAD 1.20, and groceries reflecting the country's agricultural strength. With an average annual income of CAD 19,000, Canadians balanced budgets carefully but still made room for life's small pleasures. Minimum wage hovered around CAD 3.50 per hour, giving younger workers a start. Whether it was a backyard barbecue or a day on the rink, Canadians cherished the simple moments that made life feel abundant.

Australia – Battling Inflation with Grit and Determination

Down under, Australians in 1982 faced rising inflation and unemployment, yet their resilience shone brightly. A new home in urban areas cost about AUD 50,000, and a liter of petrol was 50 cents—a fair price for traversing the vast, sunburnt country. Grocery staples like bread at 54 cents and milk kept dinner tables full, even as families adjusted their spending to meet economic challenges. Average weekly earnings for full-time adults hovered around AUD 300, ensuring most households maintained a sense of stability. Whether cheering at a cricket match or enjoying a beach picnic, Australians embraced life's simple pleasures, proving that even in difficult times, community and optimism carried them through.

Japan – Efficiency Meets Modern Living

In 1982, Japan was riding a wave of economic growth, fueled by technological advancements and export dominance. Urban living came with its costs: rent in bustling cities like Tokyo averaged ¥50,000 per month, while a liter of gasoline was about ¥150. A loaf of bread, priced at ¥130, reflected Japan's blend of affordability and quality. The average annual salary for workers was roughly ¥3,500,000, giving families the means to enjoy modern conveniences while saving for the future. Japan's meticulous attention to efficiency and innovation was evident not just in its economy but in daily life —whether in the affordability of public transportation or the variety of goods found in convenience stores. Despite rising living costs, Japan's commitment to blending tradition with modernity made 1982 a year marked by both balance and progress.

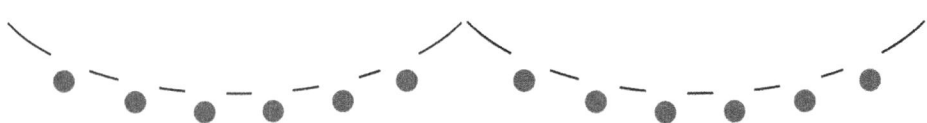

Russia – The Soviet Union's Controlled Economy

Life in the Soviet Union in 1982 was shaped by state control and scarce consumer goods. Rent was heavily subsidized, with urban apartments costing as little as 15-20 rubles per month, but availability was limited, leading to long housing waiting lists. Basic groceries were inexpensive but often hard to find. A loaf of bread cost about 20 kopeks, while a kilogram of sugar was roughly 1 ruble. Gasoline was cheap at just 20 kopeks per liter, yet private car ownership was a rare privilege, as most citizens depended on the Soviet Union's extensive and reliable public transportation network.

Wages averaged 200 rubles per month for urban workers, offering a modest lifestyle. Soviet citizens focused on practical spending, with most income devoted to necessities. Despite these constraints, education and healthcare remained free, reflecting the state's emphasis on social welfare. For many in the Soviet Union, 1982 was marked by frugality, routine, and the constant challenges of living under a planned economy.

China – A Nation on the Brink of Reform

In 1982, China stood at the dawn of profound economic transformation, with Deng Xiaoping's reforms starting to reshape the nation. The cost of living was low, but incomes remained modest. Urban workers earned an average monthly wage of 50-60 yuan, while rural farmers largely depended on subsistence farming and the collective system. A kilogram of rice cost around 0.20 yuan, and a loaf of bread about 0.30 yuan. Urban rent was minimal, often 5-10 yuan per month, as housing was usually provided by work units. Private car ownership was virtually nonexistent, and bicycles dominated transportation, with a sturdy Flying Pigeon bike costing 150 yuan—a considerable investment for many families.

CHAPTER 8

NOTABLE BIRTHS AND DEATHS IN 1982

8.1 Famous Figures Born in 1982

Lil Wayne – A Lyrical Prodigy Is Born

On September 27, 1982, Dwayne Michael Carter Jr., later known as Lil Wayne, was born in New Orleans, Louisiana. From an early age, his natural gift for storytelling and rhythm was undeniable. By nine, he was already rapping, becoming the youngest member of Cash Money Records. Lil Wayne would go on to redefine hip-hop, blending intricate lyrics with a distinctive voice that resonated across generations. Hits like "Lollipop" and albums such as Tha Carter III secured his place as one of the most influential rappers of his era.

Kirsten Dunst – Hollywood's Golden Girl

Born on April 30, 1982, Kirsten Dunst grew up in New Jersey before making her Hollywood debut at just six years old. Her breakout performance in Interview with the Vampire (1994) as the eternally youthful Claudia revealed a depth far beyond her years, earning her critical acclaim. Over time, Kirsten became a household name, starring in iconic films like Bring It On and Sam Raimi's Spider-Man trilogy. Her seamless ability to move between comedy and drama cemented her reputation as one of Hollywood's most versatile and enduring talents.

Nicki Minaj – The Queen of Rap

On December 8, 1982, Onika Tanya Maraj, better known as Nicki Minaj, was born in Saint James, Trinidad and Tobago. She moved to Queens, New York, as a child, where her bold personality and artistic flair began to flourish. Nicki shattered barriers as a female rapper, blending dynamic flows, clever wordplay, and larger-than-life alter egos. Hits like "Super Bass" and "Anaconda" not only topped charts but also cemented her as a trailblazer in the music industry, inspiring countless new artists to follow her fearless and innovative path.

Eddie Redmayne – The British Star with a Golden Touch

On January 6, 1982, Edward John David Redmayne was born in London, England. With his striking features and natural charisma, Eddie soon made a name for himself on both stage and screen. His portrayal of Stephen Hawking in The Theory of Everything earned him an Academy Award for Best Actor, highlighting his remarkable range and dedication to his craft. From historical dramas to magical adventures in Fantastic Beasts and Where to Find Them, Eddie's career stands as a testament to the enduring power of talent and unwavering commitment.

Priyanka Chopra – From Bollywood to Global Stardom

On July 18, 1982, Priyanka Chopra entered the world in Jamshedpur, India, born to a family of doctors and early expectations of a medical future. But destiny had other plans. Her Miss World crown in 2000 opened doors to Bollywood stardom, where she dazzled in films like Fashion and Barfi!. Her leap to Hollywood in Quantico and Baywatch marked her global rise. Yet her legacy isn't just cinematic—through her advocacy for gender equality and work with UNICEF, Priyanka became more than a star—she became a voice that echoed far beyond the spotlight.

Anne Hathaway – America's Sweetheart with Range

Born on November 12, 1982, in Brooklyn, New York, Anne Hathaway seemed destined for stardom. She won hearts as Mia Thermopolis in The Princess Diaries, a role that made her an instant favorite. Her rise continued with The Devil Wears Prada and Les Misérables, the latter earning her an Academy Award. Balancing box-office hits with heartfelt performances, Anne became more than just a star—she became a symbol of grace, talent, and lasting connection with audiences around the world.

8.2 Icons We Lost: Tribute to Legends

Grace Kelly – Hollywood's Princess and Monaco's Star

On September 14, 1982, the world grieved the heartbreaking loss of Grace Kelly, the luminous actress who became Princess of Monaco. With her serene beauty and poise, she captivated audiences in classics like Rear Window and To Catch a Thief. At her peak, she left Hollywood behind to serve Monaco with dignity and compassion. Her tragic death in a car accident stunned the world, yet her legacy lives on—as a timeless icon of elegance, grace, and quiet strength.

John Belushi – A Comedic Force Gone Too Soon

John Belushi, one of comedy's most electric talents, passed away on March 5, 1982, at just 33. Bursting with energy and raw charisma, he helped launch Saturday Night Live, creating unforgettable characters like the unpredictable samurai and the unforgettable Bluto from Animal House. His turn in The Blues Brothers made him a legend. Though his time was brief, his impact was lasting—Belushi's wild spirit and fearless humor still echo through the halls of comedy, a flame that burned brilliantly and far too fast.

Ayn Rand –
The Philosopher of Individualism

On March 6, 1982, the world bid farewell to Ayn Rand, the Russian-American writer and philosopher whose bold ideas sparked decades of debate. Through The Fountainhead and Atlas Shrugged, she championed Objectivism, a philosophy rooted in individualism and rational self-interest. Her words challenged readers to examine freedom, responsibility, and purpose. Though often divisive, Rand's influence on literature and thought endures—a lasting imprint of a mind unafraid to stand firmly by its convictions.

Ingrid Bergman – A Cinematic Legend Bids Farewell

On August 29, 1982, the world bid farewell to Ingrid Bergman, the luminous Swedish actress whose grace, intelligence, and quiet strength lit up the silver screen. From her iconic role in Casablanca to her Academy Award-winning performances in Gaslight and Anastasia, Bergman captivated audiences with a rare blend of vulnerability and resilience. She passed away on her 67th birthday, a poignant end to a remarkable life. Her legacy lives on in every frame she touched—timeless, moving, and forever part of cinematic history.

Henry Fonda –
The Patriarch of American Cinema

HHenry Fonda, a towering figure of Hollywood's golden age, passed away on August 12, 1982, at the age of 77. Across five remarkable decades, he brought quiet strength and profound integrity to roles in films like The Grapes of Wrath and 12 Angry Men. With his calm intensity and unwavering moral presence, Fonda became the conscience of the screen for an entire generation. His legacy lives on—not only in the timeless films he left behind, but also in the artistry of his children, Jane and Peter, who continued the Fonda tradition with grace, courage, and enduring talent.

Romy Schneider – Europe's Enigmatic Star

On May 29, 1982, the world bid farewell to Romy Schneider, the Austrian-born actress whose magnetic presence left an indelible mark on cinema. She first captured hearts as Empress Elisabeth in the beloved Sissi trilogy, then evolved into a powerful force in European drama. Though her life was touched by sorrow, her devotion to acting never wavered. Gone too soon at 43, Schneider's legacy lives on in every role shaped by her grace and strength.

Marty Robbins – The Voice of Country Music

Country music lost one of its greatest storytellers when Marty Robbins passed away on December 8, 1982. With his rich baritone and vivid songwriting, Robbins gifted the world unforgettable classics like El Paso and Big Iron. His songs, filled with love, longing, and frontier adventure, resonated across generations and touched countless hearts. Offstage, he chased speed as a passionate NASCAR driver, reflecting his bold and restless spirit. Inducted into the Country Music Hall of Fame, Robbins left more than melodies—he left a legacy of stories that still echo through every heartfelt note and verse.

CHAPTER 9

THROUGH THE EYES OF YOUTH: MEMORIES FROM 1982

The Atari 2600 – Gaming Comes Home

In 1982, the Atari 2600 reigned as the crown jewel of home entertainment, captivating kids and teens across the globe. This groundbreaking console brought the thrill of arcade hits like Space Invaders and Pac-Man into living rooms everywhere. Its joystick became an icon of a new digital age, as families huddled around glowing screens for pixel-filled adventures. More than just a machine, the Atari sparked a lifelong passion for gaming—and opened the door to countless digital dreams.

The Rubik's Cube – A Puzzle for the Ages

For kids drawn to puzzles and patterns, the Rubik's Cube was the ultimate test. This vibrant 3D brainteaser, which swept across the globe, found its place in classrooms, backpacks, and bedside tables. Children and adults alike spent countless hours twisting and turning, chasing the perfect alignment of all six sides. Whether solved in seconds or never completed, the cube became more than a toy—it was a quiet symbol of patience, focus, and determination.

He-Man and the Masters of the Universe
Heroes in the Living Room

Action figures were a childhood cornerstone in 1982, and none captured imaginations quite like He-Man and the Masters of the Universe. Inspired by the animated series, these toys transformed living rooms into the battle-scarred world of Eternia. Kids raised plastic swords high, shouting "I have the power!" as He-Man clashed with Skeletor and his evil crew. More than just molded plastic, these figures fueled endless adventures, becoming vessels of imagination and heroes in the hands of young dreamers everywhere.

My Little Pony – Magical Friends for Life

Hasbro's My Little Pony line trotted onto the scene in 1982, bringing a pastel world of ponies with flowing manes and whimsical symbols. For countless children, these ponies were more than toys—they were trusted friends. Whether brushing manes or dreaming up meadow adventures, My Little Pony inspired nurturing play and imagination, leaving a legacy of love, creativity, and childhood wonder.

G.I. Joe – Real American Heroes

In 1982, G.I. Joe made a bold comeback with smaller, more poseable action figures that captured imaginations everywhere. These 3.75-inch heroes, each with unique military roles, invited kids into worlds of daring missions and battlefield adventures. From skydives to rescues, G.I. Joe wasn't just a toy—it was a gateway to courage, creativity, and endless backyard heroism.

LEGO – Building Dreams Brick by Brick

In 1982, LEGO remained a childhood favorite, captivating young builders with sets ranging from medieval castles to futuristic space stations. With only a box of bricks and boundless imagination, kids became architects, inventors, and dreamers. More than a toy, LEGO was a creative companion —teaching problem-solving, spatial skills, and patience, all while turning living room floors into worlds of endless possibility and joy.

Care Bears – Spreading Love and Kindness

Originally born from greeting cards, the Care Bears made their plush debut in 1982, quickly becoming beloved companions for children everywhere. With unique "belly badges" and heartfelt traits, each bear taught lessons in empathy, kindness, and understanding. From Tenderheart's love to Grumpy's honesty, these soft, colorful friends brought comfort during childhood's ups and downs—and their gentle message of caring still echoes across generations.

Smurf Figurines – Bringing a Village to Life

In 1982, the Smurfs leapt from television screens into children's hands, with tiny blue figurines capturing the magic of the beloved cartoon. From wise Papa Smurf to sweet Smurfette, these toys let kids recreate the charm of Smurf Village— mushroom houses, giggles, and all. More than collectibles, Smurfs became companions in childhood adventures, inspiring creativity, storytelling, and joyful moments shared across bedrooms and living rooms around the world.

CHAPTER 10

FAMOUS WEDDINGS IN 1982

Ozzy Osbourne and Sharon Arden: A Rock and Roll Love Story

On July 4, 1982, the island of Maui, Hawaii, set the scene for a love story that would defy expectations. British rock icon Ozzy Osbourne married his manager, Sharon Arden, in a quiet ceremony far removed from heavy metal's chaos. Their bond, tested by life's storms, became the heart of both their careers and home.

Even now, Ozzy and Sharon's enduring partnership stands as a testament to lasting love amid life's loudest moments.

142

Bono and Ali Hewson: High School Sweethearts Forever

On August 21, 1982, U2's soulful frontman Bono married his high school sweetheart, Alison "Ali" Stewart, at All Saints Church in Raheny, Ireland. Their wedding was modest, echoing the sincerity of their love. As Bono's star rose, their bond remained steady—rooted in shared values, family, and a deep sense of purpose. Through decades of change and challenge, Ali has remained his anchor, showing that even amid the roar of fame, quiet, enduring love can thrive.

Marie Osmond and Steve Craig: A Love That Came Full Circle

On June 26, 1982, America's sweetheart Marie Osmond married basketball player Steve Craig in a widely celebrated ceremony that charmed fans of her music and television shows. With her radiant smile and wholesome image, Marie's wedding felt like a fairy tale. Though they divorced in 1985, love had other plans—they remarried in 2011, reminding us that sometimes, the heart finds its way home again.

Sally Ride and Steven Hawley: A Union Among the Stars

On July 24, 1982, NASA's pioneering astronauts Sally Ride and Steven Hawley exchanged vows in Salina, Kansas—a quiet moment shared by two dreamers destined for greatness. Their marriage, though later ending in divorce, symbolized a union rooted in exploration and purpose. As spacefarers and scientists, their individual contributions continue to light the way for generations inspired by courage, discovery, and the vast wonder of the unknown.

Jackie Chan and Lin Feng-jiao: A Private Love in the Spotlight

On December 1, 1982, martial arts legend Jackie Chan quietly married Taiwanese actress Lin Feng-jiao in Los Angeles. Choosing privacy over publicity, they built a life away from the spotlight, raising their son Jaycee while navigating the demands of fame. Their enduring bond is a testament to quiet devotion, proving that love can thrive even in the whirlwind of show business.

Michael Keaton and Caroline McWilliams: A Hollywood Pairing

On June 5, 1982, Michael Keaton, celebrated for his sharp wit and charisma, married actress Caroline McWilliams. United by a shared passion for acting, they inspired each other's craft. Though their marriage ended in 1990, their years together reflected the tender, often complex journey of love in the ever-shifting world of Hollywood fame.

John Malkovich and Glenne Headly: A Theatrical Union

On August 2, 1982, acclaimed actors John Malkovich and Glenne Headly married, uniting two passionate souls devoted to the arts. Their partnership, both personal and creative, left a lasting mark on stage and screen. Though their marriage ended in 1988, their artistry and shared legacy continue to be cherished by fans worldwide.

Andy Taylor and Tracy Wilson: Love Amidst the Duran Duran Craze

As Duran Duran soared to global fame, guitarist Andy Taylor married hairstylist and photographer Tracy Wilson on July 29, 1982, in Los Angeles. Their wedding blended quiet intimacy with the glamor of the moment. Amid the whirlwind of stardom, their bond reflected how love could offer stability in a world constantly spinning.

Robert Goulet and Vera Novak: A Partnership in Life and Work

On October 17, 1982, legendary singer and actor Robert Goulet wed Vera Novak—his manager, partner, and steadfast companion—in Las Vegas, Nevada. Their union blended romance with professional harmony, forming a bond rooted in trust and shared vision. Together, they crafted a legacy where love and collaboration moved in perfect step, both onstage and off.

ANSWER

Chapter 1:

1. B) The Falklands War

2. C) A massacre

3. C) Tamper-proof packaging

4. C) Air Florida Flight 90

5. B) Beaune coach crash

6. A) IRA

7. B) Kenner, Louisiana

8. A) Khalid Islambouli

9. A) Javier Pérez de Cuéllar

10. B) Equal Rights Amendment

11. C) Household Responsibility System

12. B) Signing of the Constitution Act

13. B) Greenham Common Peace Camp

14. C) Leonid Brezhnev

15. B) Vietnam Veterans Memorial

Chapter 2:

1. B) E.T. the Extra-Terrestrial
2. B) He's a replicant hunter
3. B) Gandhi
4. A) An isolated Antarctic research station
5. B) Pretends to be a woman
6. B) A Pontiac Trans Am
7. B) Cheers
8. A) St. Elsewhere
9. B) Fraggle Rock
10. C) A melancholic piano tune

Chapter 3: Answers:

1. B) Eye of the Tiger
2. A) Ebony and Ivory
3. A) Come On Eileen
4. B) Its fusion of rock and world music elements
5. B) Prince
6. C) The Message
7. B) Billie Jean
8. B) I Love Rock 'n' Roll
9. C) Africa
10. C) Madonna

Chapter 4: Answer

1. E 2. B 3. D 4. G 5. I 6. A 7. F 8. C 9. H 10. J

Chapter 5:

1. B) Oversized, padded shoulders
2. B) Their bleached and marbled appearance
3. B) Parachute pants
4. B) Leg warmers and leotards
5. B) Vibrancy and drama
6. B) Jelly shoes
7. B) They dominated everything from clothing to accessories.
8. B) "Nothing comes between me and my Calvins."
9. B) Futuristic and asymmetrical
10. B) Voluminous, teased hair with bangs
11. B) Bold blue eyeshadow and bright blush
12. A) Nostalgia for simpler times
13. B) Spandex leggings paired with sweatshirts
14. A) They were waterproof, colorful, and affordable.

1982

A LIFE TO REMEMBER

A WARM FAREWELL

Thank you for accompanying us on this fascinating journey through the year 1982. Whether it was a nostalgic revisit or a brand-new discovery, we hope it brought you joy and a sense of connection. Your passion motivates us to keep history vibrant and engaging.

Printed in Dunstable, United Kingdom